Bible Promises for WOMEN

D0173839

B&H
PUBLISHING GROUP
NASHVILLE, TENNESSEE

Bible Promises for Women
Copyright © 2003 by B&H Publishing Group
Updated and Reprinted, 2008
All Rights Reserved

ISBN: 978-0-8054-4769-9
B & H Publishing Group
Nashville, Tennessee
www.BHPublishingGroup.com

All Scripture verses are taken from the Holman
Christian Standard Bible®, Copyright © 1999,
2000, 2002, 2003 by Holman Bible Publishers.

Dewey Decimal Classification: 242.643
Women / God—Promises / Devotional Litera-
ture

Printed in the United States of America
1 2 3 4 5 12 11 10 09 08

Table of Contents

PROMISES *for* YOUR DAILY NEEDS

Your Need for Simplicity.............................. 2
Your Need for Quiet 8
Your Need for Contentment......................... 14
Your Need for Security................................. 20
Your Need for Understanding 26

PROMISES *for* YOUR FAMILY

Raising Your Children 34
Giving Them Instruction 40
Matters of the Heart 46
Portraits of Marriage 52

PROMISES *for* THE WAY YOU FEEL

When You Feel Overwhelmed 60
When You Feel Frustrated 66
When You Feel Depressed........................... 72
When You Feel Angry 78
When You Feel Regretful 84

PROMISES *for* YOUR LIFE

The Gift of Prayer 92
The Embrace of Love 98
The Power of Praise 104
The Blessings of Gratitude 110
The Joy of Living 116

Promises FOR Your Daily Needs

Much of the Bible was written almost before writing began, yet somehow the words feel like they came in on the morning bus.

They speak to needs that are as current as our last conscious thought, yet near to the heart of women throughout history.

When we ask God to meet our needs, we are speaking to One who has heard this same cry countless times across cultures and time zones, yet who never tires of handling its minutest details. We who are faithfully in His Word today are also safe in His hands.

Your Need
FOR
Simplicity

Does Life Have to Be This Complicated?

Don't worry about anything, but in everything, through prayer and petition with thanksgiving, let your requests be made known to God.

And the peace of God, which surpasses every thought, will guard your hearts and your minds in Christ Jesus.

—*Philippians 4:6–7*

Peace I leave with you. My peace I give to you. I do not give to you as the world gives. Your heart must not be troubled or fearful.
—*John 14:27*

The Spirit Himself testifies together with our spirit that we are God's children, and if children, also heirs—heirs of God and co-heirs with Christ—seeing that we suffer with Him so that we may also be glorified with Him.

For I consider that the sufferings of this present time are not worth comparing with the glory that is going to be revealed to us.
—*Romans 8:16–18*

This is why I tell you: Don't worry about your life, what you will eat or what you will drink; or about your body, what you will wear. Isn't life more than food and the body more than clothing?

Look at the birds of the sky: they don't sow or reap or gather into barns, yet your heavenly Father feeds them. Aren't you worth more than they?
—*Matthew 6:25–26*

No one can be a slave of two masters, since either he will hate one and love the other, or be devoted to one and despise the other. You cannot be slaves of God and of money.
—*Matthew 6:24*

And why do you worry about clothes? Learn how the wildflowers of the field grow: they don't labor or spin thread. Yet I tell you that not even Solomon in all his splendor was adorned like one of these!

If that's how God clothes the grass of the field, which is here today and thrown into the furnace tomorrow, won't He do much more for you—you of little faith?
—*Matthew 6:28–30*

Come to Me, all you who are weary and burdened, and I will give you rest. Take My yoke upon you and learn from Me, because I am gentle and humble in heart, and you will find rest for yourselves.
—*Matthew 11:28–29*

One day [Jesus] and His disciples got into a boat. . . . They set out, and as they were sailing He fell asleep. Then a fierce windstorm came down on the lake; they were being swamped and were in danger. They came and woke Him up, saying, "Master, Master, we're going to die!" Then He got up and rebuked the wind and the raging waves. So they ceased, and there was a calm. He said to them, "Where is your faith?" They were fearful and amazed, asking one another, "Who can this be? He commands even the winds and the waves, and they obey Him!"

—Luke 8:22–25

The Bible gives me a deep, comforting sense that things seen are temporal, and things unseen are eternal.

—Helen Keller

Now the end of all things is near; therefore, be clear-headed and disciplined for prayer.

Above all, keep your love for one another at full strength, since love covers a multitude of sins. Be hospitable to one another without complaining.

Based on the gift they have received, everyone should use it to serve others, as good managers of the varied grace of God.

If anyone speaks, his speech should be like the oracles of God; if anyone serves, his service should be from the strength God provides, so that in everything God may be glorified through Jesus Christ. To Him belong the glory and the power forever and ever. Amen.

—*1 Peter 4:7–11*

A Sabbath rest remains, therefore, for God's people. For the person who has entered His rest has rested from his own works, just as God did from His.

—*Hebrews 4:9–10*

"I am the bread of life," Jesus told them. "No one who comes to Me will ever be hungry, and no one who believes in Me will ever be thirsty again."

—*John 6:35*

Then Jesus spoke to them again: "I am the light of the world. Anyone who follows Me will never walk in the darkness but will have the light of life."

—*John 8:12*

I am afflicted and needy;
    the LORD thinks of me.
You are my help and my deliverer;
    my God, do not delay.

—*Psalm 40:17*

Your Need
FOR
Quiet

Help Me to Slow Down, to Be Still

The result of righteousness will be peace;
    the effect of righteousness
    will be quiet confidence forever.
Then my people will dwell in a peaceful place,
    and in safe and restful dwellings.
      —*Isaiah 32:17–18*

I said, "If only I had wings like a dove!
    I would fly away and find rest.
How far away I would flee;
    I would stay in the wilderness.
I would hurry to my shelter
    from the raging wind and the storm."
        —*Psalm 55:6–8*

This is what the LORD says:
    "Stand by the roadways and look.
Ask about the ancient paths:
    Which is the way to what is good?
    Then take it and find rest for yourselves.
        —*Jeremiah 6:16a*

The Lord GOD, the Holy One of Israel,
has said: "You will be delivered by returning
and resting; your strength will lie in quiet
confidence."
        —*Isaiah 30:15a*

Calmness puts great offenses to rest.
        —*Ecclesiastes 10:4b*

When I observe Your heavens,
 the work of Your fingers,
the moon and the stars,
 which You set in place,
what is man that You remember him,
 the son of man that You look after him?
You made him little less than God
 and crowned him with glory and honor.
   —Psalm 8:3–5

The LORD is good to those who wait for Him,
 to the person who seeks Him.
It is good to wait quietly
 for deliverance from the LORD.
   —Lamentations 3:25–26

LORD, my heart is not proud;
 my eyes are not haughty.
I do not get involved with things
 too great or too difficult for me.
Instead, I have calmed and quieted myself
 like a little weaned child with its mother;
 I am like a little child.
   —Psalm 131:1–2

Trust in the LORD and do what is good;
    dwell in the land and live securely.
Take delight in the LORD,
    and He will give you your heart's desires.
Commit your way to the LORD;
    trust in Him, and He will act,
making your righteousness shine like the dawn,
    your justice like the noonday.
Be silent before the LORD
    and wait expectantly for Him.
      —Psalm 37:3–7a

The Bible is God's message to everybody. We
deceive ourselves if we claim to want to hear
His voice but neglect the primary channel
through which it comes.
    —Elisabeth Elliot

Sing for joy, Daughter Zion;
>   shout loudly, Israel!
Be glad and rejoice with all your heart,
>   Daughter Jerusalem!
The LORD has removed your punishment;
>   He has turned back your enemy.
The King of Israel, the LORD, is among you;
>   you need no longer fear harm.
On that day it will be said to Jerusalem:
>   "Do not fear;
>   Zion, do not let your hands grow weak.
The LORD your God is among you,
>   a warrior who saves.
He will rejoice over you with gladness.
>   He will bring you quietness with His love.
>   He will delight in you with shouts of joy.
>   —*Zephaniah 3:14–17*

On the last and most important day of the festival, Jesus stood up and cried out, "If anyone is thirsty, he should come to Me and drink! The one who believes in Me, as the Scripture has said, will have streams of living water flow from deep within him."
—*John 7:37–38*

Let us go to His dwelling place;
    let us worship at His footstool.
Arise, Lord, come to Your resting place,
    You and the ark that shows Your strength.
May Your priests be clothed
    with righteousness,
    and may Your godly people shout for joy.
—*Psalm 132:7–9*

Finally brothers, whatever is true, whatever is honorable, whatever is just, whatever is pure, whatever is lovely, whatever is commendable—if there is any moral excellence and if there is any praise—dwell on these things.
—*Philippians 4:8*

Your Need
FOR
Contentment

I Can Be Happy with This, Can't I?

Though the fig tree does not bud
    and there is no fruit on the vines,
though the olive crop fails
    and the fields produce no food,
though there are no sheep in the pen
    and no cattle in the stalls,
yet I will triumph in the LORD;
    I will rejoice in the God of my salvation!
    —Habakkuk 3:17–18

When I am filled with cares,
    Your comfort brings me joy.
        —*Psalm 94:19*

For He crushes but also binds up;
    He strikes, but His hands also heal.
        —*Job 5:18*

Let us strive to know the LORD.
    His appearance is as sure as the dawn.
He will come to us like the rain,
    like the spring showers that water the land.
        —*Hosea 6:3*

I will give praise in the great congregation
    because of You;
I will fulfill my vows
    before those who fear You.
The humble will eat and be satisfied;
    those who seek the LORD will praise Him.
        —*Psalm 22:25–26a*

Your life should be free from the love of money. Be satisfied with what you have, for He Himself has said, I will never leave you or forsake you.

—*Hebrews 13:5*

If you ever forget the LORD your God and go after other gods to worship and bow down to them, I testify against you today that you will perish.

—*Deuteronomy 8:19*

But godliness with contentment is a great gain. For we brought nothing into the world, and we can take nothing out. But if we have food and clothing, we will be content with these.

But those who want to be rich fall into temptation, a trap, and many foolish and harmful desires, which plunge people into ruin and destruction. For the love of money is a root of all kinds of evil, and by craving it, some have wandered away from the faith and pierced themselves with many pains.

—*1 Timothy 6:6–10*

Two things I ask of You;
    don't deny them to me before I die:
Keep falsehood and
    deceitful words far from me.
Give me neither poverty nor wealth;
    feed me with the food I need.
Otherwise, I might have too much
    and deny You, saying, "Who is the LORD?"
or I might have nothing and steal,
    profaning the name of my God.
      —Proverbs 30:7–9

    The Bible belongs to those elemental things—like the sky, the wind, and the sea, like the kisses of little children and tears shed beside the grave—which can never grow stale or out of date.
      — T. H. Darlow

Remember this: the person who sows sparingly will also reap sparingly, and the person who sows generously will also reap generously. . . .

And God is able to make every grace overflow to you, so that in every way, always having everything you need, you may excel in every good work.

As it is written: "He has scattered; He has given to the poor; His righteousness endures forever."

Now the One who provides seed for the sower and bread for food will provide and multiply your seed and increase the harvest of your righteousness, as you are enriched in every way for all generosity, which produces thanksgiving to God through us.

—*2 Corinthians 9:6, 8–11*

Blessed are those who hunger and thirst for righteousness, because they will be filled.
—*Matthew 5:6*

How long will I store up
    anxious concerns within me,
    agony in my mind every day? . . .
But I have trusted in Your faithful love;
    my heart will rejoice in Your deliverance.
I will sing to the LORD
    because He has treated me generously.
—*Psalm 13:2a, 5–6*

Do not be agitated by evildoers;
    do not envy those who do wrong.
For they wither quickly like grass
    and wilt like tender green plants.
—*Psalm 37:1–2*

The fear of the LORD leads to life;
    one will sleep at night without danger.
—*Proverbs 19:23*

Your Need

FOR

Security

I Want to Trust You, Lord, for Everything

I keep the LORD in mind always.
 Because He is at my right hand,
 I will not be shaken.
Therefore my heart is glad,
 and my spirit rejoices;
 my body also rests securely. . . .
You reveal the path of life to me;
 in Your presence is abundant joy;
 in Your right hand are eternal pleasures.
 —*Psalm 16:8–9, 11*

The LORD is my light and my salvation—
    whom should I fear?
The LORD is the stronghold of my life—
    of whom should I be afraid?
    —*Psalm 27:1*

When I am afraid,
    I will trust in You.
In God, whose word I praise,
    in God I trust; I will not fear.
    What can man do to me?
    —*Psalm 56:3–4*

We have this kind of confidence toward God through Christ: not that we are competent in ourselves to consider anything as coming from ourselves, but our competence is from God.
    —*2 Corinthians 3:4–5*

Therefore if the Son sets you free, you really will be free.
    —*John 8:36*

Your heart must not be troubled. Believe in God; believe also in Me. In My Father's house are many dwelling places; if not, I would have told you. I am going away to prepare a place for you. If I go away and prepare a place for you, I will come back and receive you to Myself, so that where I am you may be also.
—*John 14:1–3*

All who came before Me are thieves and robbers, but the sheep didn't listen to them. I am the door. If anyone enters by Me, he will be saved and will come in and go out and find pasture. A thief comes only to steal and to kill and to destroy. I have come that they may have life and have it in abundance.
—*John 10:8–10*

I will take you to be My wife forever.
　　I will take you to be
　　My wife in righteousness,
　　justice, love, and compassion.
I will take you to be My wife in faithfulness,
　　and you will know the LORD.
—*Hosea 2:19–20*

The LORD is good,
    a stronghold in a day of distress;
    He cares for those who take refuge in Him.
        —*Nahum 1:7*

He will stand and shepherd them
    in the strength of Yahweh,
    in the majestic name of Yahweh His God.
They will live securely,
    for then His greatness will extend
    to the ends of the earth.
        —*Micah 5:4*

We need to study the Bible intelligently, not as if the Scriptures were a sort of holy rabbit's foot, but for its wisdom in the broad sweep of its teaching about the nature of God and of man.
        —*Catherine Marshall*

The LORD is my shepherd;
  there is nothing I lack.
He lets me lie down in green pastures;
  He leads me beside quiet waters.
He renews my life;
  He leads me along the right paths
  for His name's sake.
Even when I go through the darkest valley,
  I fear no danger,
for You are with me;
  Your rod and Your staff—they comfort me.
You prepare a table before me
  in the presence of my enemies;
You anoint my head with oil;
  my cup overflows.
Only goodness and faithful love will pursue me
  all the days of my life,
and I will dwell in the house of the LORD
  as long as I live.
      —*Psalm 23:1–6*

I will leave a meek and
      humble people among you,
      and they will trust in the name of Yahweh.
            —*Zephaniah 3:12*

The name of the LORD is a strong tower;
      the righteous run to it and are protected.
            —*Proverbs 18:10*

You will keep in perfect peace
      the mind that is dependent on You,
      for it is trusting in You.
Trust in the LORD forever,
      because in Yah, the LORD,
      is an everlasting rock!
            —*Isaiah 26:3–4*

Now may the God of hope fill you with
all joy and peace in believing, so that you may
overflow with hope by the power of the Holy
Spirit.
            —*Romans 15:13*

Your Need
FOR
Understanding

I Believe, Lord, but . . . Help My Unbelief

I pray that the eyes of your heart may be enlightened so you may know what is the hope of His calling, what are the glorious riches of His inheritance among the saints, and what is the immeasurable greatness of His power to us who believe, according to the working of His vast strength.

—*Ephesians 1:18–19*

I have written these things to you who believe in the name of the Son of God, so that you may know that you have eternal life.
—*1 John 5:13*

And we know that the Son of God has come and has given us understanding so that we may know the true One. We are in the true One—that is, in His Son Jesus Christ. He is the true God and eternal life.
—*1 John 5:20*

You love Him, though you have not seen Him. And though not seeing Him now, you believe in Him and rejoice with inexpressible and glorious joy, because you are receiving the goal of your faith, the salvation of your souls.
—*1 Peter 1:8–9*

This is the victory that has conquered the world: our faith. And who is the one who conquers the world but the one who believes that Jesus is the Son of God?
—*1 John 5:4b–5*

Dear friends, do not believe every spirit, but test the spirits to determine if they are from God, because many false prophets have gone out into the world.

This is how you know the Spirit of God: Every spirit who confesses that Jesus Christ has come in the flesh is from God. But every spirit who does not confess Jesus is not from God. . . .

You are from God, little children, and you have conquered them, because the One who is in you is greater than the one who is in the world.

—*1 John 4:1–3a, 4*

Therefore we will not be afraid,
    though the earth trembles
and the mountains topple
    into the depths of the seas.
        —*Psalm 46:2*

This saying is trustworthy and deserves full acceptance. In fact, we labor and strive for this, because we have put our hope in the living God.

—*1 Timothy 4:9–10a*

Therefore, I will most gladly boast all the more about my weaknesses, so that Christ's power may reside in me. . . . For when I am weak, then I am strong.
—*2 Corinthians 12:9b, 10b*

For our momentary light affliction is producing for us an absolutely incomparable eternal weight of glory. So we do not focus on what is seen, but on what is unseen; for what is seen is temporary, but what is unseen is eternal.
—*2 Corinthians 4:17–18*

It is as silly for a Christian to set out upon the journey of life without the Bible to guide them as it is for a traveler to set off without a map.
—*Jill Briscoe*

Therefore, brothers, since we have boldness to enter the sanctuary through the blood of Jesus, by the new and living way that He has inaugurated for us, through the curtain (that is, His flesh); and since we have a great high priest over the house of God, let us draw near with a true heart in full assurance of faith, our hearts sprinkled clean from an evil conscience and our bodies washed in pure water.

Let us hold on to the confession of our hope without wavering, for He who promised is faithful. . . .

My righteous one will live by faith; and if he draws back, My soul has no pleasure in him. But we are not those who draw back and are destroyed, but those who have faith and obtain life.

—*Hebrews 10:19–23. 38–39*

So don't throw away your confidence, which has a great reward. For you need endurance, so that after you have done God's will, you may receive what was promised.
—*Hebrews 10:35–36*

Before this faith came, we were confined under the law, imprisoned until the coming faith was revealed.
—*Galatians 3:23*

But our citizenship is in heaven, from which we also eagerly wait for a Savior, the Lord Jesus Christ. He will transform the body of our humble condition into the likeness of His glorious body, by the power that enables Him to subject everything to Himself.
—*Philippians 3:20–21*

Now the God of all grace, who called you to His eternal glory in Christ Jesus, will personally restore, establish, strengthen, and support you after you have suffered a little.
—*1 Peter 5:10*

Promises FOR Your Family

You are defined in many ways. Yet it's within your family relationships—as a daughter, perhaps as a wife and mother—that you carry the greatest weight of trust and obligation, as well as the potential for your greatest joys.

As a daughter, you bear the responsibility of honoring your parents, gratefully loving and receiving love. As a wife, you have become the tender guardian of a man's heart, the faithful bearer of his dreams. As a mom, you have become the light in a child's morning, the smile that can turn tears to laughter. In all your family roles, you are a giver of blessing.

Raising
YOUR
Children

Don't They Come with Directions?

Children, obey your parents in the Lord, because this is right. Honor your father and mother—which is the first commandment with a promise— that it may go well with you and that you may have a long life in the land.
—*Ephesians 6:1–3*

Teach a youth about the way he should go;
   even when he is old
   he will not depart from it.
      —*Proverbs 22:6*

Let Your work be seen by Your servants,
   and Your splendor by their children.
      —*Psalm 90:16*

Tell your children about it,
   and let your children tell their children,
   and their children the next generation.
      —*Joel 1:3*

Walk as children of light—for the fruit of the light results in all goodness, righteousness, and truth—discerning what is pleasing to the Lord.
      —*Ephesians 5:8b–10*

Therefore, be imitators of God, as dearly loved children. And walk in love, as the Messiah also loved us and gave Himself for us, a sacrificial and fragrant offering to God.
      —*Ephesians 5:1–2*

Come, children, listen to me;
> I will teach you the fear of the LORD.

Who is the man who delights in life,
> loving a long life to enjoy what is good?

Keep your tongue from evil
> and your lips from deceitful speech.

Turn away from evil and do what is good;
> seek peace and pursue it.
>> —*Psalm 34:11–14*

In the fear of the LORD
> one has strong confidence
> and his children have a refuge.
>> —*Proverbs 14:26*

My little children, I am writing you these things so that you may not sin. But if anyone does sin, we have an advocate with the Father—Jesus Christ the righteous One.
> —*1 John 2:1*

For we have become companions of the Messiah if we hold firmly until the end the reality that we had at the start.
> —*Hebrews 3:14*

Don't withhold correction from a youth.
—*Proverbs 23:13a*

Discipline your son, and he will give you comfort; he will also give you delight.
—*Proverbs 29:17*

Little children, we must not love in word or speech, but in deed and truth.
—*1 John 3:18*

Whatever merit there is in anything that I have written is simply due to the fact that when I was a child, my mother daily read me a part of the Bible and made me learn a part of it by heart.
—*John Ruskin*

Therefore, get your minds ready for action, being self-disciplined, and set your hope completely on the grace to be brought to you at the revelation of Jesus Christ.

As obedient children, do not be conformed to the desires of your former ignorance but, as the One who called you is holy, you also are to be holy in all your conduct; for it is written, "Be holy, because I am holy."

And if you address as Father the One who judges impartially based on each one's work, you are to conduct yourselves in reverence during this time of temporary residence. . . .

For "all flesh is like grass, and all its glory like a flower of the grass. The grass withers, and the flower drops off, but the word of the Lord endures forever." And this is the word that was preached as the gospel to you.

—*1 Peter 1:13–17, 24–25*

See that you don't look down on one of these little ones, because I tell you that in heaven their angels continually view the face of My Father in heaven. . . .

What do you think? If a man has 100 sheep, and one of them goes astray, won't he leave the 99 on the hillside and go and search for the stray? And if he finds it, I assure you: He rejoices over that sheep more than over the 99 that did not go astray.

In the same way, it is not the will of your Father in heaven that one of these little ones perish.

—*Matthew 18:10, 12–14*

Whoever welcomes one little child such as this in My name welcomes Me.

—*Mark 9:37a*

I am not seeking what is yours, but you. For children are not obligated to save up for their parents, but parents for their children. I will most gladly spend and be spent for you.

—*2 Corinthians 12:14b–15a*

Giving
THEM
Instruction

I Want Them to Know God Loves Them

Go around Zion, encircle it;
    count its towers,
note its ramparts; tour its citadels
    so that you can tell a future generation:
"This God, our God forever and ever—
    He will lead us eternally."
        —*Psalm 48:12–14*

I will declare wise sayings;
 I will speak mysteries from the past—
things we have heard and known
 and that our fathers have passed down to us.
We must not hide them from their children,
 but must tell a future generation
the praises of the LORD,
 His might, and the wonderful works
 He has performed.
He established a testimony in Jacob
 and set up a law in Israel,
which He commanded our fathers
 to teach to their children
so that a future generation—
 children yet to be born—might know.
They were to rise and tell their children
 so that they might put
 their confidence in God
and not forget God's works,
 but keep His commandments.
 —Psalm 78:2–7

Command your children to carefully
follow all the words of this law. For they are
not meaningless words to you but they are
your life.
 —Deuteronomy 32:46b–47a

There is no one righteous, not even one.
—*Romans 3:10b*

But when the goodness and love for man
appeared from God our Savior, He saved
us—not by works of righteousness that we had
done, but according to His mercy, through the
washing of regeneration and renewal by the
Holy Spirit . . . so that having been justified by
His grace, we may become heirs with the hope
of eternal life.

This saying is trustworthy. I want you
to insist on these things, so that those who
have believed God might be careful to devote
themselves to good works. These are good and
profitable for everyone.
—*Titus 3:4–5, 7–8*

Then we will no longer be little children,
tossed by the waves and blown around by
every wind of teaching, by human cunning
with cleverness in the techniques of deceit. But
speaking the truth in love, let us grow in every
way into Him who is the head—Christ.
—*Ephesians 4:14–15*

Listen and hear my voice.
   Pay attention and hear what I say.
      —*Isaiah 28:23*

I pray that you, being rooted and firmly
established in love, may be able to comprehend
with all the saints what is the breadth and
width, height and depth, and to know the Messiah's love that surpasses knowledge, so you
may be filled with all the fullness of God.
      —*Ephesians 3:17b–19*

We must never lose sight of the fact that
the Bible is not a single book. The Bible is,
strictly speaking, not a book but a library.
      —*Frederic William Farrar*

Get wisdom, get understanding;
    don't forget or turn away
    from the words of my mouth.
Don't abandon wisdom,
    and she will watch over you;
    love her, and she will guard you.
Wisdom is supreme—so get wisdom.
    And whatever else you get,
    get understanding.
Cherish her, and she will exalt you;
    if you embrace her,
    she will honor you.
She will place a garland
    of grace on your head;
she will give you
    a crown of beauty.
        —*Proverbs 4:5–9*

Your word is a lamp for my feet.
  —*Psalm 119:105a*

But be doers of the word and not hearers
only, deceiving yourselves. Because if anyone is
a hearer of the word and not a doer, he is like
a man looking at his own face in a mirror; for
he looks at himself, goes away, and right away
forgets what kind of man he was.

But the one who looks intently into the
perfect law of freedom and perseveres in it,
and is not a forgetful hearer but a doer who
acts—this person will be blessed in what
he does.
  —*James 1:22–25*

My son, if your heart is wise,
  my heart will indeed rejoice.
My innermost being will cheer
  when your lips say what is right.
Don't be jealous of sinners;
  instead, always fear the LORD.
For then you will have a future,
  and your hope will never fade.
  —*Proverbs 23:15–18*

Matters
OF THE
Heart

Help Me Remember What's Really Important

Impress these words of Mine on your hearts.
. . . Teach them to your children, talking about
them when you sit in your house and when you
walk along the road, when you lie down and
when you get up. Write them on the doorposts
of your house and on your gates, so that as long
as the heavens are above the earth, your days
and those of your children may be many.
—*Deuteronomy 11:18a, 19–21a*

Be on your guard and diligently watch yourselves, so that you don't forget the things your eyes have seen and so that they don't slip from your mind as long as you live. Teach them to your children and your grandchildren.
—*Deuteronomy 4:9*

And I pray this: that your love will keep on growing in knowledge and every kind of discernment, so that you can determine what really matters and can be pure and blameless in the day of Christ, filled with the fruit of righteousness that comes through Jesus Christ, to the glory and praise of God.
—*Philippians 1:9–11*

This is how we know that we love God's children when we love God and obey His commands. For this is what love for God is: to keep His commands. Now His commands are not a burden, because whatever has been born of God conquers the world.
—*1 John 5:2–4a*

Love must be without hypocrisy. Detest evil; cling to what is good. Show family affection to one another with brotherly love. Outdo one another in showing honor. Do not lack diligence; be fervent in spirit; serve the Lord.

Rejoice in hope; be patient in affliction; be persistent in prayer. Share with the saints in their needs; pursue hospitality. Bless those who persecute you; bless and do not curse. Rejoice with those who rejoice; weep with those who weep.

Be in agreement with one another. Do not be proud; instead, associate with the humble. Do not be wise in your own estimation. Do not repay anyone evil for evil. Try to do what is honorable in everyone's eyes. If possible, on your part, live at peace with everyone.

—*Romans 12:9–18*

Practice these things; be committed to them, so that your progress may be evident to all. Be conscientious about yourself and your teaching; persevere in these things, for by doing this you will save both yourself and your hearers.

—*1 Timothy 4:15–16*

For I desire loyalty and not sacrifice,
  the knowledge of God
  rather than burnt offerings.
    —*Hosea 6:6*

You do not want a sacrifice, or I would give it;
  You are not pleased with a burnt offering.
The sacrifice pleasing to God is a broken spirit.
  God, You will not despise
  a broken and humbled heart.
    —*Psalm 51:16–17*

Have not our suspicious hearts darkened
this Book of light? Do we not often read it as
the proclamation of a command to do, instead
of a declaration of what the love of God has
done?
    —*Horatio Bonar*

For this reason also, since the day we heard this, we haven't stopped praying for you.

We are asking that you may be filled with the knowledge of His will in all wisdom and spiritual understanding, so that you may walk worthy of the Lord, fully pleasing to Him, bearing fruit in every good work and growing in the knowledge of God.

May you be strengthened with all power, according to His glorious might, for all endurance and patience, with joy giving thanks to the Father, who has enabled you to share in the saints' inheritance in the light.

He has rescued us from the domain of darkness and transferred us into the kingdom of the Son He loves, in whom we have redemption, the forgiveness of sins.

—*Colossians 1:9–14*

Just as I have loved you, you must also love one another. By this all people will know that you are My disciples, if you have love for one another.

—John 13:34b–35

"This is the most important," Jesus answered: "'Listen, Israel! The Lord our God, The Lord is One. Love the Lord your God with all your heart, with all your soul, with all your mind, and with all your strength.' The second is: 'Love your neighbor as yourself.' There is no other commandment greater than these."

—Mark 12:29–31

This saying is trustworthy and deserving of full acceptance: "Christ Jesus came into the world to save sinners"—and I am the worst of them. But I received mercy because of this, so that in me, the worst of them, Christ Jesus might demonstrate the utmost patience as an example to those who would believe in Him for eternal life.

—1 Timothy 1:15–16

Portraits

OF

Marriage

This Is the Kind of Wife I Want to Be

Who can find a capable wife?
    She is far more precious than jewels.
The heart of her husband trusts in her,
    and he will not lack anything good.
She rewards him with good, not evil,
    all the days of her life.
        —*Proverbs 31:10–12*

My love calls to me:
"Arise, my darling.
Come away, my beautiful one.
For now the winter is past;
the rain has ended and gone away.
The blossoms appear in the countryside.
The time of singing has come,
and the turtledove's cooing
is heard in our land.
The fig tree ripens its figs;
the blossoming vines
give off their fragrance.
Arise, my darling.
Come away, my beautiful one."
—Song of Songs 2:10–13

Like a lily among thorns,
so is my darling among the young women.
—Song of Songs 2:2

My love is mine and I am his.
—Song of Songs 2:16a

This is my love, and this is my friend.
—Song of Songs 5:16b

Wives, in the same way, submit yourselves to your own husbands so that, even if some disobey the Christian message, they may be won over without a message by the way their wives live, when they observe your pure, reverent lives.

—*1 Peter 3:1–2*

Marriage must be respected by all, and the marriage bed kept undefiled, because God will judge immoral people and adulterers.

—*Hebrews 13:4*

For this is God's will, your sanctification: that you abstain from sexual immorality, so that each of you knows how to possess his own vessel in sanctification and honor.

—*1 Thessalonians 4:3–4*

He who created them in the beginning "made them male and female," and He also said: "For this reason a man will leave his father and mother and be joined to his wife, and the two will become one flesh."

—*Matthew 19:4–5*

Your beauty should not consist of outward things like elaborate hairstyles and the wearing of gold ornaments or fine clothes; instead, it should consist of the hidden person of the heart with the imperishable quality of a gentle and quiet spirit, which is very valuable in God's eyes.
—*1 Peter 3:3–4*

A house and wealth are inherited from fathers, but a sensible wife is from the LORD.
—*Proverbs 19:14*

The highest earthly enjoyments are but a shadow of the joy I find in reading God's Word.
—*Lady Jane Grey*

She extends her hands to the spinning staff,
and her hands hold the spindle.
Her hands reach out to the poor,
and she extends her hands to the needy.
She is not afraid for her household
when it snows, for all in her
household are doubly clothed.
She makes her own bed coverings;
her clothing is fine linen and purple.
Her husband is known at the city gates,
where he sits among the elders of the land.
She makes and sells linen garments;
she delivers belts to the merchants.
Strength and honor are her clothing,
and she can laugh at the time to come.
She opens her mouth with wisdom,
and loving instruction is on her tongue.
She watches over the activities
of her household and is never idle.
—*Proverbs 31:19–27*

She selects wool and flax
   and works with willing hands.
She is like the merchant ships,
   bringing her food from far away.
She rises while it is still night
   and provides food for her household
   and portions for her servants.
She evaluates a field and buys it;
   she plants a vineyard with her earnings.
She draws on her strength
   and reveals that her arms are strong.
She sees that her profits are good,
   and her lamp never goes out at night.
   —*Proverbs 31:13–18*

Her sons rise up and call her blessed.
   Her husband also praises her:
"Many women are capable,
   but you surpass them all!"
Charm is deceptive and beauty is fleeting,
   but a woman who
   fears the LORD will be praised.
Give her the reward of her labor,
   and let her works
   praise her at the city gates.
   —*Proverbs 31:28–31*

Promises FOR THE Way You Feel

Emotions don't play fair. They don't need a reason to show up, just an excuse. But tricky and evasive as they are, feelings still have to be dealt with. Discerned. Disarmed.

That's when the sword of truth becomes our most trusted weapon—the sharp knife of reality that can cut through all the chattering and complaining until God's way becomes clear and our feelings come under control. In the Word of God our emotions find room to be expressed and heard, but also find reasons to be distrusted and held accountable.

WHEN YOU FEEL
Overwhelmed

I Just Can't Seem to Get It All Done

God, hear my cry;
   pay attention to my prayer.
I call to You from the ends of the earth
   when my heart is without strength.
Lead me to a rock that is high above me,
   for You have been a refuge for me,
   a strong tower in the face of the enemy.
   —*Psalm 61:1–3*

I cry aloud to the LORD;
    I plead aloud to the LORD for mercy.
I pour out my complaint before Him;
    I reveal my trouble to Him.
Although my spirit is weak within me,
    You know my way.
      —Psalm 142.1–3a

You guide me with Your counsel,
    and afterwards You will
    take me up in glory.
Whom do I have in heaven but You?
    And I desire nothing on earth but You.
My flesh and my heart may fail,
    but God is the strength of my heart,
    my portion forever.
      —Psalm 73:24–26

I love You, LORD,
    my strength.
The LORD is my rock,
    my fortress, and my deliverer,
my God, my mountain where I seek refuge,
    my shield and the horn of my salvation,
    my stronghold.
      —Psalm 18:1–2

Has God forgotten to be gracious?
    Has He in anger withheld
    His compassion?". . . .
I will remember the LORD's works;
    yes, I will remember Your ancient wonders.
I will reflect on all You have done
    and meditate on Your actions. . . .
You are the God who works wonders;
    You revealed Your strength
    among the peoples.
        —*Psalm 77:9, 11–12, 14*

God, You are my God; I eagerly seek You.
    I thirst for You;
my body faints for You
    in a land that is dry,
    desolate, and without water.
So I gaze on You in the sanctuary
    to see Your strength and Your glory.
My lips will glorify You
    because Your faithful love
    is better than life.
So I will praise You as long as I live;
    at Your name, I will lift up my hands.
You satisfy me as with rich food;
    my mouth will praise You with joyful lips.
        —*Psalm 63:1–5*

LORD, You are my lamp;
    the LORD illuminates my darkness.
With You I can attack a barrier,
    and with my God I can leap over a wall. . . .
For who is God besides the LORD?
    And who is a rock? Only our God.
God is my strong refuge;
    He makes my way perfect.
        —2 Samuel 22:29–30, 31–32

The pledged word of God to man is no puffball to break at a touch and scatter into dust. It is iron. It is gold, the most malleable of metals. It is more golden than gold. It abides imperishable forever.
    —Amy Carmichael

Finally, be strengthened by the Lord and by His vast strength. Put on the full armor of God so that you can stand against the tactics of the Devil.

For our battle is not against flesh and blood, but against the rulers, against the authorities, against the world powers of this darkness, against the spiritual forces of evil in the heavens.

This is why you must take up the full armor of God, so that you may be able to resist in the evil day, and having prepared everything, to take your stand. . . .

In every situation take the shield of faith, and with it you will be able to extinguish the flaming arrows of the evil one. Take the helmet of salvation, and the sword of the Spirit, which is God's word.

—*Ephesians 6:10–13, 16–17*

For although we are walking in the flesh, we do not wage war in a fleshly way, since the weapons of our warfare are not fleshly, but are powerful through God for the demolition of strongholds. We demolish arguments and every high-minded thing that is raised up against the knowledge of God, taking every thought captive to the obedience of Christ.

—*2 Corinthians 10:3–5*

Do not fear, for I have redeemed you; I have called you by your name; you are Mine. I will be with you when you pass through the waters, and when you pass through the rivers, they will not overwhelm you. You will not be scorched when you walk through the fire, and the flame will not burn you. For I am the LORD your God, the Holy One of Israel, and your Savior.

—*Isaiah 43:1b–3a*

When you walk,
  your steps will not be hindered;
  when you run, you will not stumble.

—*Proverbs 4:12*

WHEN YOU FEEL
Frustrated

Who Makes Sure My Needs Are Met?

Why do you assert: "My way is hidden from the LORD, and my claim is ignored by my God"?

Do you not know? Have you not heard? Yahweh is the everlasting God, the Creator of the whole earth. He never grows faint or weary; there is no limit to His understanding. He gives strength to the weary and strengthens the powerless.

—*Isaiah 40:27b–29*

Dear friends, when the fiery ordeal arises among you to test you, don't be surprised by it, as if something unusual were happening to you. Instead, as you share in the sufferings of the Messiah rejoice, so that you may also rejoice with great joy at the revelation of His glory.

—*1 Peter 4:12–13*

Consider it a great joy, my brothers, whenever you experience various trials, knowing that the testing of your faith produces endurance. But endurance must do its complete work, so that you may be mature and complete, lacking nothing.

—*James 1:2–4*

Therefore, brothers, by the mercies of God, I urge you to present your bodies as a living sacrifice, holy and pleasing to God; this is your spiritual worship. Do not be conformed to this age, but be transformed by the renewing of your mind, so that you may discern what is the good, pleasing, and perfect will of God.

—*Romans 12:1–2*

You know that those who are regarded as rulers of the Gentiles dominate them, and their men of high positions exercise power over them. But it must not be like that among you.

On the contrary, whoever wants to become great among you must be your servant, and whoever wants to be first among you must be a slave to all. For even the Son of Man did not come to be served, but to serve, and to give His life—a ransom for many.

—Mark 10:42–45

The one who loves his life will lose it, and the one who hates his life in this world will keep it for eternal life.

—John 12:25

If anyone wants to come with Me, he must deny himself, take up his cross daily, and follow Me. For whoever wants to save his life will lose it, but whoever loses his life because of Me will save it.

—Luke 9:23–24

Carry one another's burdens; in this way you will fulfill the law of Christ. For if anyone considers himself to be something when he is nothing, he is deceiving himself. But each person should examine his own work, and then he will have a reason for boasting in himself alone, and not in respect to someone else. For each person will have to carry his own load.

—*Galatians 6:2–5*

The Bible reveals God's soul to us in a way that no other book is able to do. It is a gospel tract, distilling the essence of our relationship to the Lord, but it is also an epic, introducing us to the immensity of an eternal God.

—*Joni Eareckson Tada*

I raise my eyes toward the mountains.
    Where will my help come from?
My help comes from the LORD,
    the Maker of heaven and earth.
He will not allow your foot to slip;
    your Protector will not slumber.
Indeed, the Protector of Israel
    does not slumber or sleep.
The LORD protects you;
    the LORD is a shelter right by your side.
The sun will not strike you by day,
    or the moon by night.
The LORD will protect you from all harm;
    He will protect your life.
The LORD will protect your coming and going
    both now and forever.
        —*Psalm 121:1–8*

Dear friends, if our hearts do not condemn us we have confidence before God, and can receive whatever we ask from Him because we keep His commands and do what is pleasing in His sight.

Now this is His command: that we believe in the name of His Son Jesus Christ, and love one another as He commanded us. The one who keeps His commands remains in Him, and He in him. And the way we know that He remains in us is from the Spirit He has given us.

—*1 John 3:21–24*

For me, living is Christ.
—*Philippians 1:21a*

So don't worry, saying, "What will we eat?" or "What will we drink?" or "What will we wear?" For the idolaters eagerly seek all these things, and your heavenly Father knows that you need them.

But seek first the kingdom of God and His righteousness, and all these things will be provided for you.
—*Matthew 6:31–33*

WHEN YOU FEEL
Depressed

I Can Feel Myself Sinking Again

My soul, praise the LORD,
    and do not forget all His benefits.
He forgives all your sin;
    He heals all your diseases.
He redeems your life from the Pit;
    He crowns you with
    faithful love and compassion.
He satisfies you with goodness;
    your youth is renewed like the eagle.
      —*Psalm 103:2–5*

Why has my pain become unending,
    my wound incurable,
    refusing to be healed?
You truly have become like a mirage to me—
    water that is not reliable.
      —Jeremiah 15:18

You have distanced loved one
    and neighbor from me;
    darkness is my only friend.
      —Psalm 88:18

Do not rejoice over me, my enemy!
    Though I have fallen, I will stand up;
though I sit in darkness,
    the Lord will be my light.
      —Micah 7:8

For the Lord
    will not reject us forever.
Even if He causes suffering,
    He will show compassion
    according to His abundant, faithful love.
For He does not enjoy bringing affliction
    or suffering on mankind.
      —Lamentations 3:31–33

The ropes of death were wrapped around me,
and the torments of Sheol overcame me;
I encountered trouble and sorrow.
Then I called on the name of the LORD:
"LORD, save me!"
The LORD is gracious and righteous;
our God is compassionate.
The LORD guards the inexperienced;
I was helpless, and He saved me.
Return to your rest, my soul,
for the LORD has been good to you.
For You, LORD, rescued me from death,
my eyes from tears,
my feet from stumbling.
I will walk before the LORD
in the land of the living.
I believed, even when I said,
"I am severely afflicted."
In my alarm I said,
"Everyone is a liar."
How can I repay the LORD
all the good He has done for me?
I will take the cup of salvation
and worship the LORD.
I will fulfill my vows to the LORD
in the presence of all His people.
—*Psalm 116:3–14*

On that day I will respond—
    the LORD'S declaration. . . .
I will sow her in the land for Myself,
    and I will have compassion
    on No Compassion;
I will say to Not My People:
    You are My people,
    and he will say: You are My God.
        —Hosea 2:21a, 23

There have been times when I have only
been capable of reading a few verses at a time,
yet the supernatural, life-giving power of the
Word of God has given me strength to go on,
even if only one day at a time.
        —Anne Graham Lotz

The waters engulfed me up to the neck;
    the watery depths overcame me. . . .
I sank to the foundations of the mountains;
    the earth with its prison bars
    closed behind me forever!
But You raised my life from the Pit,
    LORD my God!
As my life was fading away,
    I remembered the LORD.
My prayer came to You,
    to Your holy temple.
Those who cling to worthless idols
    forsake faithful love,
but as for me, I will sacrifice to You
    with a voice of thanksgiving.
I will fulfill what I have vowed.
    Salvation is from the LORD!
      —Jonah 2:5a, 6–9

Lord, my every desire is known to You;
   my sighing is not hidden from You.
    —*Psalm 38:9*

I have asked one thing from the LORD;
   it is what I desire:
to dwell in the house of the LORD
   all the days of my life,
gazing on the beauty of the LORD
   and seeking Him in His temple.
For He will conceal me in His shelter
   in the day of adversity;
He will hide me under the cover of His tent;
   He will set me high on a rock.
Then my head will be high
   above my enemies around me;
I will offer sacrifices in His tent
   with shouts of joy.
   I will sing and make music to the LORD.
    —*Psalm 27:4–6*

For God has not given us a spirit of fearfulness, but one of power, love, and sound judgment.
    —*2 Timothy 1:7*

WHEN YOU FEEL
Angry

I've Been So Upset with Everyone Lately

Who perceives his unintentional sins?
　　Cleanse me from my hidden faults.
Moreover, keep Your servant from willful sins;
　　do not let them rule over me. . . .
May the words of my mouth
　　and the meditation of my heart
be acceptable to You,
　　LORD, my rock and my Redeemer.
　　　　—*Psalm 19:12–13a, 14*

Refrain from anger and give up your rage;
  do not be agitated—it can only bring harm.
    —*Psalm 37:8*

"Be angry and do not sin." Don't let the
sun go down on your anger, and don't give the
Devil an opportunity.
    —*Ephesians 4:26–27*

For it is God's will that you, by doing
good, silence the ignorance of foolish people.
    —*1 Peter 2:15*

A gentle answer turns away anger,
  but a harsh word stirs up wrath.
    —*Proverbs 15:1*

My dearly loved brothers, understand this:
everyone must be quick to hear, slow to speak,
and slow to anger, for man's anger does not
accomplish God's righteousness.
    —*James 1:19–20*

Each one of us must please his neighbor for his good, in order to build him up.

For even the Messiah did not please Himself. On the contrary, as it is written, "The insults of those who insult You have fallen on Me."
—*Romans 15:2–3*

Therefore, God's chosen ones, holy and loved, put on heartfelt compassion, kindness, humility, gentleness, and patience, accepting one another and forgiving one another if anyone has a complaint against another. Just as the Lord has forgiven you, so also you must forgive.

Above all, put on love—the perfect bond of unity. And let the peace of the Messiah, to which you were also called in one body, control your hearts. Be thankful.

Let the message about the Messiah dwell richly among you, teaching and admonishing one another in all wisdom, and singing psalms, hymns, and spiritual songs, with gratitude in your hearts to God.
—*Colossians 3:12–16*

And whatever you do, in word or in deed, do everything in the name of the Lord Jesus, giving thanks to God the Father through Him.
—*Colossians 3:17*

Speak and act as those who will be judged by the law of freedom. For judgment is without mercy to the one who hasn't shown mercy. Mercy triumphs over judgment.
—*James 2:12–13*

It has been well said that upsetting the Bible is like upsetting a solid cube of granite; it is just as big one way as the other, and when you have upset it, it is right side up, and when you overturn it, it is right side up still.
—*David F. Nygren*

I say to you who listen: Love your enemies, do good to those who hate you, bless those who curse you, pray for those who mistreat you.

If anyone hits you on the cheek, offer the other also. And if anyone takes away your coat, don't hold back your shirt either. Give to everyone who asks from you, and from one who takes away your things, don't ask for them back. Just as you want others to do for you, do the same for them.

If you love those who love you, what credit is that to you? Even sinners love those who love them. If you do what is good to those who are good to you, what credit is that to you? Even sinners do that. And if you lend to those from whom you expect to receive, what credit is that to you? Even sinners lend to sinners to be repaid in full.

But love your enemies, do what is good, and lend, expecting nothing in return. Then your reward will be great, and you will be sons of the Most High. For He is gracious to the ungrateful and evil.

—*Luke 6:27–35*

Now finally, all of you should be like-minded and sympathetic, should love believers, and be compassionate and humble, not paying back evil for evil or insult for insult but, on the contrary, giving a blessing, since you were called for this, so that you can inherit a blessing.
—*1 Peter 3:8–9*

No rotten talk should come from your mouth, but only what is good for the building up of someone in need, in order to give grace to those who hear. . . . All bitterness, anger and wrath, insult and slander must be removed from you, along with all wickedness. And be kind and compassionate to one another, forgiving one another, just as God also forgave you in Christ.
—*Ephesians 4:29, 31–32*

Now may the God of endurance and encouragement grant you agreement with one another, according to Christ Jesus, so that you may glorify the God and Father of our Lord Jesus Christ with a united mind and voice.
—*Romans 15:5–6*

WHEN YOU FEEL
Regretful

Where Can I Go to Start Over?

I will give you a new heart and put a new spirit within you; I will remove your heart of stone and give you a heart of flesh. I will place My Spirit within you and cause you to follow My statutes and carefully observe My ordinances.

—*Ezekiel 36:26–27*

Blessed are the poor in spirit,
    because the kingdom of heaven is theirs.
Blessed are those who mourn,
    because they will be comforted.
Blessed are the gentle,
    because they will inherit the earth.
    —*Matthew 5:3–5*

Lord, if You considered sins,
    Lord, who could stand?
But with You there is forgiveness,
    so that You may be revered.
I wait for the Lord; I wait,
    and put my hope in His word.
I wait for the Lord
    more than watchmen for the morning—
    more than watchmen for the morning.
    —*Psalm 130:3–6*

That is how we will know we are of the
truth, and will convince our hearts in His presence, because if our hearts condemn us, God is
greater than our hearts and knows all things.
    —*1 John 3:19–20*

Say to the faint–hearted:
    "Be strong; do not fear!
Here is your God; vengeance is coming.
    God's retribution is coming;
    He will save you."....
Then the lame will leap like a deer,
    and the tongue
    of the mute will sing for joy,
for water will gush in the wilderness,
    and streams in the desert;
the parched ground
    will become a pool of water,
    and the thirsty land springs of water....
A road will be there and a way;
    it will be called the Holy Way.
The unclean will not travel on it,
    but it will be for him who walks the path.
    Even the fool will not go astray....
But the redeemed will walk on it,
    and the ransomed of the LORD will return
and come to Zion with singing,
    crowned with unending joy.
Joy and gladness will overtake them,
    and sorrow and sighing will flee.
      —Isaiah 35:4, 6–7a, 8, 9b–10

Godly grief produces a repentance not to be regretted and leading to salvation. . . . For consider how much diligence this very thing—this grieving as God wills—has produced in you: what a desire to clear yourselves, what indignation, what fear, what deep longing, what zeal, what justice! In every way you have commended yourselves to be pure in this matter.
—*2 Corinthians 7:10a, 11*

To know and embrace and live by God's Word is to know and embrace and live by Him; it is to build that solid, unshakable structure that will keep you from collapsing in the rubble of disappointment's earthquakes.
—*Kay Arthur*

You have said this: "Our transgressions and our sins are heavy on us, and we are wasting away because of them! How then can we survive?"

Tell them: "As I live"—the declaration of the Lord GOD—"I take no pleasure in the death of the wicked, but rather that the wicked person should turn from his way and live. . . .

"So when I tell the wicked person: You will surely die, but he repents of his sin and does what is just and right—he returns collateral, makes restitution for what he has stolen, and walks in the statutes of life without practicing iniquity—he will certainly live; he will not die.

"None of the sins he committed will be held against him. He has done what is just and right; he will certainly live."

—*Ezekiel 33:10b–11a, 14–16*

As a mother comforts her son,
    so I will comfort you,
    and you will be comforted in Jerusalem.
      —Isaiah 66:13

I greatly rejoice in the LORD,
    I exult in my God;
for He has clothed me
    with the garments of salvation
    and wrapped me in a robe of righteousness,
as a bridegroom wears a turban
    and as a bride adorns herself with her jewels.
      —Isaiah 61:10

Go and eat what is rich, drink what is
sweet, and send portions to those who have
nothing prepared, since today is holy to our
Lord. Do not grieve, because your strength
comes from rejoicing in the LORD.
      —Nehemiah 8:10

Promises
FOR
Your Life

Every woman has her ups and downs, her good days and her bad days, her moments of rest and her bouts with worry.

So surely you've known days when the wind blows cold, when the walls close in, when the nearest escape is nowhere in sight. But even in the most trying times—when you really take the time to listen—you can still feel the brush of God's presence, the warm wrap of His love, the comfort of knowing He's still in control. And remind yourself that you are still one of His finest creations.

The Gift

OF

Prayer

Lord, I'm Glad You Can Hear Me

Let me experience
    Your faithful love in the morning,
    for I trust in You.
Reveal to me the way I should go,
    because I long for You.
Rescue me from my enemies, LORD;
    I come to You for protection.
Teach me to do Your will,
    for You are my God.
        —*Psalm 143:8–10a*

Now this is the confidence we have before Him: whenever we ask anything according to His will, He hears us. And if we know that He hears whatever we ask, we know that we have what we have asked Him for.

—*1 John 5:14–15*

Keep asking, and it will be given to you. Keep searching, and you will find. Keep knocking, and the door will be opened to you.

—*Matthew 7:7*

When you pray, don't babble like the idolaters, since they imagine they'll be heard for their many words. Don't be like them, because your Father knows the things you need before you ask Him.

—*Matthew 6:7–8*

Therefore let us approach the throne of grace with boldness, so that we may receive mercy and find grace to help us at the proper time.

—*Hebrews 4:16*

I cry aloud to God,
   aloud to God, and He will hear me.
In my day of trouble I sought the Lord.
   My hands were lifted up all night long.
      —*Psalm 77:1–2*

The LORD is near all who call out to Him,
   all who call out to Him with integrity.
He fulfills the desires of those who fear Him;
   He hears their cry for help and saves them.
      —*Psalm 145:18–19*

You will pray to Him, and He will hear you,
   and you will fulfill your vows.
When you make a decision,
   it will be carried out,
   and light will shine on your ways.
      —*Job 22:27–28*

Be gracious to me, Lord,
   for I call to You all day long.
For You, Lord, are kind and ready to forgive,
   abundant in faithful love
   to all who call on You.
      —*Psalm 86:3, 5*

May the name of God
  be praised forever and ever,
  for wisdom and power belong to Him.
He changes the times and seasons;
  He removes kings and establishes kings.
He gives wisdom to the wise
  and knowledge to those
  who have understanding.
He reveals the deep and hidden things.
  He knows what is in the darkness,
  and light dwells with Him.
  —*Daniel 2:20–22*

God has handed us two sticks of dynamite
with which to demolish our strongholds: His
Word and prayer. What is more powerful than
two sticks of dynamite placed in separate loca-
tions? Two strapped together.
  —*Beth Moore*

Come and see the works of God;
    His acts toward mankind
    are awe-inspiring. . . .
Come and listen, all who fear God,
    and I will tell what He has done for me.
I cried out to Him with my mouth,
    and praise was on my tongue.
If I had been aware of malice in my heart,
    the Lord would not have listened.
However, God has listened;
    He has paid attention
    to the sound of my prayer.
May God be praised!
    He has not turned away my prayer
    or turned His faithful love from me.
      —Psalm 66:5, 16–20

Now if any of you lacks wisdom, he should ask God, who gives to all generously and without criticizing, and it will be given to him.
—*James 1:5*

Even before they call, I will answer;
    while they are still speaking, I will hear.
    —*Isaiah 65:24*

Lord my God, You have done many things—
    Your wonderful works
    and Your plans for us;
    none can compare with You.
If I were to report and speak of them,
    they are more than can be told.
    —*Psalm 40:5*

But as for me, I will look to the Lord;
    I will wait for the God of my salvation.
    My God will hear me.
    —*Micah 7:7*

The Embrace
OF
Love

Tell Me Again How Much You Love Me

Look at how great a love the Father has given us, that we should be called God's children. And we are! . . .

Dear friends, we are God's children now, and what we will be has not yet been revealed. We know that when He appears, we will be like Him, because we will see Him as He is. And everyone who has this hope in Him purifies himself just as He is pure.

—*1 John 3:1a, 2–3*

Rarely will someone die for a just person—though for a good person perhaps someone might even dare to die. But God proves His own love for us in that while we were still sinners Christ died for us!

—*Romans 5:7–8*

No one has greater love than this, that someone would lay down his life for his friends.

—*John 15:13*

And we have come to know and to believe the love that God has for us. God is love, and the one who remains in love remains in God, and God remains in him.

In this, love is perfected with us so that we may have confidence in the day of judgment; for we are as He is in this world.

There is no fear in love; instead, perfect love drives out fear, because fear involves punishment. So the one who fears has not reached perfection in love. We love because He first loved us.

—*1 John 4:16–19*

Love consists in this: not that we loved God, but that He loved us and sent His Son to be the propitiation for our sins.

Dear friends, if God loved us in this way, we also must love one another.

No one has ever seen God. If we love one another, God remains in us and His love is perfected in us.

—*1 John 4:10–12*

Aren't two sparrows sold for a penny? Yet not one of them falls to the ground without your Father's consent. But even the hairs of your head have all been counted. Don't be afraid therefore; you are worth more than many sparrows.

—*Matthew 10:29–31*

You did not choose Me, but I chose you. I appointed you that you should go out and produce fruit and that your fruit should remain, so that whatever you ask the Father in My name, He will give you.

—*John 15:16*

For if, while we were enemies, we were reconciled to God through the death of His Son, then how much more, having been reconciled, will we be saved by His life! And not only that, but we also rejoice in God through our Lord Jesus Christ, through whom we have now received reconciliation.

—Romans 5:10–11

To Him who loves us and has set us free from our sins by His blood, and made us a kingdom, priests to His God and Father—to Him be the glory and dominion forever and ever.

—Revelation 1:5b–6

The Scriptures were not given to us that we should enclose them in books but engrave them upon our hearts.

—John Chrysostom

Who can separate us from the love of Christ?
    Can affliction or anguish
    or persecution or famine
    or nakedness or danger or sword? . . .
No, in all these things
    we are more than victorious
    through Him who loved us.
For I am persuaded that neither death nor life,
    nor angels nor rulers,
nor things present, nor things to come,
    nor powers, nor height, nor depth,
    nor any other created thing
will have the power to separate us
    from the love of God
    that is in Christ Jesus our Lord!
        —Romans 8:35, 37–39

I have been crucified with Christ; and I no longer live, but Christ lives in me. The life I now live in the flesh, I live by faith in the Son of God, who loved me and gave Himself for me.

—Galatians 2:19b–20

He also raised us up with Him and seated us with Him in the heavens, in Christ Jesus, so that in the coming ages He might display the immeasurable riches of His grace in His kindness to us in Christ Jesus.

—Ephesians 2:6–7

But whoever keeps His word, truly in him the love of God is perfected. This is how we know we are in Him: the one who says he remains in Him should walk just as He walked.

—1 John 2:5–6

To those who are the called, loved by God the Father and kept by Jesus Christ. May mercy, peace, and love be multiplied to you.

—Jude 1b–2

The Power

OF

Praise

Lord, You're Really Something

How unsearchable His judgments
and untraceable His ways!
For who has known the mind of the Lord?
Or who has been His counselor?
Or who has ever first given to Him,
and has to be repaid?
For from Him and through Him
and to Him are all things.
To Him be the glory forever.
—*Romans 11:33b–36*

Come, let us worship and bow down;
   let us kneel before the LORD our Maker.
For He is our God,
   and we are the people of His pasture,
   the sheep under His care.
      —*Psalm 95:6–7*

For You are my hope, Lord GOD,
   my confidence from my youth.
I have leaned on You from birth;
   You took me from my mother's womb.
   My praise is always about You.
      —*Psalm 71:5–6*

Better a day in Your courts
   than a thousand anywhere else.
I would rather be at the door
   of the house of my God
   than to live in the tents of the wicked.
For the LORD God is a sun and shield.
   The LORD gives grace and glory;
He does not withhold the good
   from those who live with integrity.
LORD of Hosts,
   happy is the person who trusts in You!
      —*Psalm 84:10–12*

Lord, You are my portion
    and my cup of blessing;
    You hold my future.
The boundary lines have fallen for me
    in pleasant places;
    indeed, I have a beautiful inheritance.
        —*Psalm 16:5–6*

For here we do not have an enduring city;
instead, we seek the one to come. Therefore,
through Him let us continually offer up to God
a sacrifice of praise, that is, the fruit of our lips
that confess His name.
        —*Hebrews 13:14–15*

Sing to the Lord,
    for He has done glorious things.
    Let this be known throughout the earth.
        —*Isaiah 12:5*

I will sing about the Lord's
    faithful love forever;
with my mouth I will proclaim
    Your faithfulness to all generations.
        —*Psalm 89:1*

You have a mighty arm;
    Your hand is powerful;
    Your right hand is lifted high.
Righteousness and justice
    are the foundation of Your throne;
    faithful love and truth go before You.
Happy are the people
    who know the joyful shout;
LORD, they walk in the light
    of Your presence.
They rejoice in Your name all day long,
    and they are exalted by Your righteousness.
    For You are their magnificent strength.
    —Psalm 89:13–17a

Scripture is not a concept; Scripture is a person. When you stand before the Word of God, you are standing face-to-face with God.
    —Henry Blackaby

Blessed be the God and Father of our Lord Jesus Christ. According to His great mercy, He has given us a new birth into a living hope through the resurrection of Jesus Christ from the dead, and into an inheritance that is imperishable, uncorrupted, and unfading, kept in heaven for you, who are being protected by God's power through faith for a salvation that is ready to be revealed in the last time.

You rejoice in this, though now for a short time you have had to be distressed by various trials so that the genuineness of your faith—more valuable than gold, which perishes though refined by fire—may result in praise, glory, and honor at the revelation of Jesus Christ.

—1 Peter 1:3–7

How good it is to sing to our God,
for praise is pleasant and lovely.
—*Psalm 147:1*

When, on my bed, I think of You,
I meditate on You during the night watches
because You are my help;
I will rejoice in the shadow of Your wings.
I follow close to You;
Your right hand holds on to me.
—*Psalm 63:6–8*

Those who know Your name trust in You
because You have not abandoned
those who seek You, LORD.
—*Psalm 9:10*

My salvation and glory depend on God;
my strong rock, my refuge, is in God.
Trust in Him at all times, you people;
pour out your hearts before Him.
God is our refuge.
—*Psalm 62:7–8*

The
Blessings
OF
Gratitude

Lord, I Just Wanted to Say Thanks

Let them give thanks to the LORD
   for His faithful love and His
   wonderful works for the human race.
For He has satisfied the thirsty
   and filled the hungry with good things.
   —*Psalm 107:8–9*

Lord, You have been our refuge
in every generation.
Before the mountains were born,
before You gave birth
to the earth and the world,
from eternity to eternity, You are God.
—*Psalm 90:1–2*

I remember the days of old;
I meditate on all You have done;
I reflect on the work of Your hands.
—*Psalm 143:5*

If Your instruction had not been my delight,
I would have died in my affliction.
I will never forget Your precepts,
for You have given me life through them.
—*Psalm 119:92–93*

Our mouths were filled with laughter then,
and our tongues with shouts of joy.
Then they said among the nations,
"The LORD has done
great things for them."
—*Psalm 126:2*

Blessed be the God and Father of our Lord Jesus Christ, who has blessed us with every spiritual blessing in the heavens, in Christ; for He chose us in Him, before the foundation of the world, to be holy and blameless in His sight.

In love He predestined us to be adopted through Jesus Christ for Himself, according to His favor and will, to the praise of His glorious grace that He favored us with in the Beloved.

In Him we have redemption through His blood, the forgiveness of our trespasses, according to the riches of His grace that He lavished on us with all wisdom and understanding.

He made known to us the mystery of His will, according to His good pleasure that He planned in Him for the administration of the days of fulfillment—to bring everything together in the Messiah, both things in heaven and things on earth in Him.

—*Ephesians 1:3–10*

For God was pleased to have all His fullness dwell in Him, and through Him to reconcile everything to Himself.
—*Colossians 1:19–20a*

But you are a chosen race, a royal priesthood,
    a holy nation, a people for His possession,
so that you may proclaim the praises
    of the One who called you out of darkness
    into His marvelous light.
Once you were not a people,
    but now you are God's people;
you had not received mercy,
    but now you have received mercy.
—*1 Peter 2:9–10*

Break thou the bread of life, dear Lord, to me / As thou didst break the loaves beside the sea / Beyond the sacred page I seek thee, Lord / My spirit pants for thee, O living Word.
—*Mary A. Lathbury*

If the LORD had not been on our side—
    let Israel say—
If the LORD had not been on our side
    when men attacked us,
then they would have swallowed us alive
    in their burning anger against us.
Then the waters would have engulfed us;
    the torrent would have swept over us;
    the raging waters would have swept over us.
Praise the LORD,
    who has not let us be
    ripped apart by their teeth.
We have escaped like a bird
    from the hunter's net;
    the net is torn, and we have escaped.
Our help is in the name of the LORD,
    the Maker of heaven and earth.

    —Psalm 124:1–8

Give thanks in everything,
    for this is God's will for you in Christ Jesus.
        —*1 Thessalonians 5:18*

I will praise the LORD at all times;
    His praise will always be on my lips.
I will boast in the LORD;
    the humble will hear and be glad.
        —*Psalm 34:1–2*

Give thanks to the LORD, for He is good;
    His faithful love endures forever.
Let the redeemed of the LORD proclaim
    that He has redeemed them
    from the hand of the foe
and has gathered them from the lands—
    from the east and the west,
    from the north and the south.
        —*Psalm 107:1–3*

My mouth will tell about Your righteousness
    and Your salvation all day long,
    though I cannot sum them up.
        —*Psalm 71:15*

The Joy
OF
Living

Just Being Here Is Such a Blessing

Children were brought to Him so He might put His hands on them and pray. But the disciples rebuked them.

Then Jesus said, "Leave the children alone, and don't try to keep them from coming to Me, because the kingdom of heaven is made up of people like this."

—*Matthew 19:13–14*

Let your father and mother have joy,
　　and let her who gave birth to you rejoice.
　　　　—*Proverbs 23:25*

Even a sparrow finds a home,
　　and a swallow, a nest for herself
where she places her young—
　　near Your altars, LORD of Hosts,
　　my King and my God.
How happy are those
　　who reside in Your house,
　　who praise You continually.
Happy are the people whose strength is in You,
　　whose hearts are set on pilgrimage.
As they pass through the Valley of Baca,
　　they make it a source of springwater.
　　　　—*Psalm 84:3–6*

　　You will eat there in the presence of the
LORD your God and rejoice with your household in everything you do, because the LORD
your God has blessed you.
　　　　—*Deuteronomy 12:7*

Sons are indeed a heritage from the LORD,
   children, a reward.
      —*Psalm 127:3*

He gives the childless woman a household,
   making her the joyful mother of children.
      —*Psalm 113:9*

I have no greater joy than this:
   to hear that my children
   are walking in the truth.
      —*3 John 4*

I have been young and now I am old,
   yet I have not seen
   the righteous abandoned
   or his children begging bread.
He is always generous, always lending,
   and his children are a blessing.
      —*Psalm 37:25–26*

   And whoever welcomes one child like this
in My name welcomes Me.
      —*Matthew 18:5*

Now if you faithfully obey the LORD your God and are careful to follow all His commands I am giving you today, the LORD your God will put you far above all the nations of the earth. All these blessings will come and overtake you, because you obey the LORD your God:

You will be blessed in the city
and blessed in the country.
Your descendants will be blessed,
and your soil's produce,
and the offspring of your livestock,
including the young of your herds
and the newborn of your flocks.
Your basket and kneading bowl
will be blessed.
You will be blessed when you come in
and blessed when you go out.
—*Deuteronomy 28:1–6*

Be careful how you live; you may be the only Bible some person ever reads.
—*W. J. Toms*

I will praise You,
    because I have been
    remarkably and wonderfully made.
Your works are wonderful,
    and I know this very well.
My bones were not hidden from You
    when I was made in secret,
when I was formed in the
    depths of the earth.
Your eyes saw me when I was formless;
    all my days were written in Your book
and planned before
    a single one of them began.
God, how difficult Your thoughts are
    for me to comprehend;
    how vast their sum is!
If I counted them,
    they would outnumber the grains of sand;
    when I wake up, I am still with You.
        —*Psalm 139:14–18*

May the LORD add to your numbers,
  both yours and your children's.
May you be blessed by the LORD,
  the Maker of heaven and earth.
The heavens are the LORD's,
  but the earth He has given
  to the human race.
It is not the dead who praise the LORD,
  nor any of those
  descending into the silence of death.
But we will praise the LORD,
  both now and forever.
    —*Psalm 115:14–18*

The LORD bless you and protect you;
  the LORD make His face shine on you,
  and be gracious to you;
the LORD look with favor on you
  and give you peace.
    —*Numbers 6:24–26*

Happy are the people with such blessings.
  Happy are the people
  whose God is the LORD.
    —*Psalm 144:15*